THE EASY THING

VICTOR PATRICK

ISBN-13: 9798857258088

ISBN-10: 1477123456

Cover design by: Art Painter

Library of Congress Control Number: 2018675309

Printed in the United States of America All rights reserved.

ISBN:

DEDICATION

This invaluable book is dedicated to God Almighty.

CONTENTS

INTRODUCTION

The Easy Thing is a subtle yet potent idea that goes unnoticed in a world that frequently celebrates the road of hard labor and hustle. Imagine leading a life in which success comes naturally and where reaching your goals doesn't necessitate constant work and sacrifice. What if I told you that the secret to unlocking this ease is within your reach? It might sound too good to be true.

Welcome to "The Easy Thing," an innovative method for attaining your goals without becoming burned out or jeopardizing your wellbeing. In this eBook, we'll explore the profound wisdom of keeping things simple along the way, going with the flow, and harnessing the amazing power of ease.

The days of constant striving and grinding in search of achievement are long gone. Instead, I invite you to set out on a life-changing quest that disproves conventional thinking and unlocks a world where success comes easily.

We will discuss useful tactics, mindset changes, and tried-and-true methods to help you escape the chains of excessive effort on the pages that follow. We'll expose the covert obstacles that have kept you trapped in a cycle of struggle and direct you toward a new paradigm in which you embrace the way that presents the least amount of difficulty and fully utilize the power of alignment and flow.

But let me be clear: choosing the simple path does not entail avoiding difficulties or avoiding development. Working smarter rather than harder is the goal. It involves coordinating your actions with your purpose and utilizing your natural abilities and qualities. Finding the sweet spot where accomplishment and ease coexist is the goal.

You'll find motivational tales of people who have discovered the secret to effortless success in their own lives throughout this eBook. Their experiences will act as lighthouses, pointing you in the direction of ease and illuminating what's possible when you change your perspective and adopt a new way of being.

Now turn the page and start your revolutionary journey if you're ready to let go of the antiquated notion that achieving success means sacrificing your happiness and well-being. Get ready to discover the keys to effortless success and design a life where doing the simple things inspires spectacular accomplishment.

Remember, it's time to embrace a life where achievement and ease go hand in hand and to rewrite the story. Let's dive in and learn more about The Easy Thing's revolutionary potential!

UNDERSTANDING FEAR AND RESISTANCE

Humans naturally experience fear and resistance in the face of uncertainty, change, and challenges. They frequently result from a fear of failing, being judged, or the unknown. These feelings have the power to immobilize us, s topping us from making the essential progress in our own develop ment and achievement.

Fear is the only thing we have to dread, according to Roosevelt, Franklin.

Sometimes the problems we face are less intimidating than our fear s and anxieties.

It is crucial to face our fears head-on if we are to get over the obstacles standing in our way.

For God did not give us a spirit of fear, but of power, love, and self-control."
- 2 Tim. 1:7.

You

possess the strength to face our fears, the love to trust in our abiliti es, and the self-control to go through challenges.

Adopting this spirit gives us the courage and will to face resistance and fear.

The Harry Potter series author, J.K. Rowling, overcame countless r ejections before her works became successful. This is her persever ance story.

Her experience shows the value of tenacity in the face of resistance and fear.

Several publishers turned Rowling down because they did not reco gnize the potential in her writing. She persisted in trying to get her writings published nonetheless, not allowing her anxiety to stop her.

The acceptance of Rowling's debut book was ultimately a result of her patience and unflinching faith in her work.

Her status as a literary legend was further cemented when the Harr y Potter book series went on to become one of the best-selling book series of all time.

Techniques for Surmounting Opposition and Fear:

- Choose the Source: consider what is causing your anxieties and resistance.

You can deal with these feelings more skillfully if you know where they come from.

- Question negative ideas and replace them with uplifting affi rmations to reframe negative thinking.

- Have a growth mentality that sees difficulties as chances fo r development.

- Start by taking modest, attainable moves in the direction of your objectives.

- Steady advancement might boost self-assurance and lessen worry.

- Get Support: Surround yourself with friends, family, or me ntors who will be there to encourage and inspire you when t hings become tough.

- See failure as a stepping stone to achievement and learn fro m setbacks.

- Use setbacks as opportunities to grow by learning from the m.

Personal development and success need overcoming opposition and fear. We may overcome fear and reluctance with the correct mindset and techniques, creating possibilities for growth and fulfilling our full potential.

<u>SIMPLIFYING COMPLEXITY</u>

Simplicity does not mean oversimplifying or dismissing complexities; instead, it means breaking complicated ideas down into smaller, more manageable parts. It enables us to more clearly understand complicated concepts, which enhances our ability to make decisions and solve problems.

"The height of sophistication is simplicity." - Leo da Vinci. True sophistication is found in simplicity. We can gain a deep understanding and elegant answers by simplifying complicated issues.

God is not a God of chaos, but of peace." Corinthians 14:33. Understand that God's preference for harmony and peace is above chaos. We link ourselves with a higher sense of harmony and purpose by pursuing simplicity.

Albert Einstein, a world-famous physicist, was remarkably adept at demystifying difficult scientific concepts. His theory of relativity revolutionized physics, and he communicated it in a way that was appealing to both academics and the general public.

In order to simplify complex ideas, Einstein used thought experiments and analogies that everyone could understand. His famous equation, $E=mc2$, captured the connection between energy, mass, and speed of light in a deceptively simple way, forever altering our understanding of the universe.

Simpler Ways to Handle Complexity

* ❖ Determine the Core Elements: Concentrate on the most important elements of a work or project and give them top priority. Decision-making is streamlined as a result, and excessive complexity is avoided.
* ❖ Speak Clearly: When communicating complicated concepts to others, use simple language and avoid using jargon or technical phrases. Better understanding and teamwork are fostered by effective communication.
* ❖ Use Visuals: To more effectively represent complex data or relationships, include visual aids like diagrams, charts, or info graphics.
* ❖ Convert difficult jobs or projects into more manageable chunks by breaking them down. One thing at a time can help the process feel less overwhelming overall.
* ❖ Adopt minimalism: Get rid of extraneous components, features, or procedures that do not significantly advance the main goal. Maintain a clear, concise focus.

The art of simplifying complexity promotes greater effectiveness, comprehension, and harmony. Accepting simplicity enables us to handle complex problems with ease and produce amazing achievements. In the quest for clarity, keep in mind that simplicity holds the key to revealing the genuine elegance and beauty of any endeavor

<u>UNDERSTANDING THE POWER OF RESILIENCE</u>

The ability to endure through difficult circumstances and come out stronger on the other side depends on the ability to be resilient. It is about accepting setbacks as stepping stones to further successes rather than about avoiding failure.

The greatest accomplishment in life is rising every time we fall, not never falling. - Mandela, Nelson. The words of Nelson Mandela serve as a reminder that true greatness is determined by our capacity to rise and carry on after each setback rather than by the absence of failures. The ability of the human spirit to endure and flourish is demonstrated through resilience.

"Consider it all joy, my brothers, when you experience trials of all kinds, because you know that the testing of your faith promotes steadfastness"- James 1:2-3. This exhorts us to rejoice in the midst of tribulations since they develop and fortify our character. Faithful perseverance develops into steadfastness, which equips us with the strength to face challenges head-on in the future.

Oprah Winfrey's life experience is a wonderful example of overcoming adversity and demonstrating perseverance. She had a difficult upbringing characterized by deprivation and abuse, but she refused to let her situation define her. Oprah moved forward due to her fierce determination and unflinching self-confidence.

Oprah persevered despite encountering various obstacles in her profession, such as early job terminations and difficulties as a talk show presenter. Through her talk show and then her media empire, OWN, she used her platform to empower and inspire millions of people around the world (Oprah Winfrey Network).

Oprah's capacity to face her previous traumas, embrace vulnerability, and use them to forge meaningful connections with people is an example of her resilience. She became one of the most well-known and successful media personalities in the world thanks to her real and authentic attitude, which won the hearts of millions of people.

Resilience-Building Techniques

Develop a growth mindset by viewing hurdles as opportunities for learning and growth rather than as insurmountable barriers.

Create Coping Mechanisms: Create a toolkit of coping techniques, such as journaling, meditation, or asking loved ones for assistance when things are tough.

Challenge Negative Self-Talk and Reframe Setbacks as Temporary and Solvable Challenges. Reframe Negative Thinking.

Establish Achievable and Realistic Goals: To prevent feeling overwhelmed and discouraged, set attainable and realistic goals.

Exercise self-compassion: Recognize that everyone suffers difficulties and treat yourself with kindness and understanding when things get tough.

The ability to develop resilience is crucial for coping with life's ups and downs. Resilience enables us to bounce back from setbacks stronger and more knowledgeable, opening the door to a life of success and fulfillment. Remember that overcoming obstacles with grace and dedication is what defines true greatness, not avoiding them.

CULTIVATING A GROWTH MINDSET

Without being constrained by prior knowledge, the beginner's mind perceives options and possibilities. By adopting a growth mindset, we can keep the wonder and curiosity of a novice, which inspires us to innovate and grow.

"Do not be conformed to this world, but be changed by the renewing of your mind -Romans 12:2. We undergo significant alteration when we renew our minds and adopt a growth mentality. This way of thinking enables us to question the status quo and look forward to a better future.

The development of the light bulb by Thomas Edison is evidence of the effectiveness of a growth mentality and unflinching determination. Edison experienced a number of setbacks and disappointments in his quest to develop a useful and durable electric light. He nevertheless saw each setback as a chance to grow and learn.

Famously, Edison once said: "I did not mess up. I recently discovered 10,000 methods that will not work." This demonstrates his tenacity and readiness to see failure as a springboard for success. By persevering with his experiments, Edison was motivated by his growth mentality to eventually succeed in developing a dependable incandescent light bulb, which revolutionized the entire world.

How to Foster a Development Mindset

- Accept Challenges: Rather than dreading failure, embrace obstacles as chances for development and learning.
- Consider Effort a Road to Mastery: Think of putting forth effort as a means of mastery rather than as a sign of inadequacy. Accept the idea that you can learn and get better.
- Acknowledge constructive criticism and use it as feedback to advance your progress.
- Appreciate Other People's Success: Instead, than feeling frightened or resentful by other people's success, celebrate it and use it as inspiration through challenges.

The secret to realizing our potential and establishing ongoing success and growth is cultivating a growth mindset. We may perceive limitless opportunities, keep going after setbacks, and change our own lives as well as the world around us when we have a growth mentality. We may continue to develop into the finest versions of ourselves by embracing the power of growth and development. Keep in mind that the path to progress starts with the regeneration of the mind and the conviction that we have an endless capacity for growth.

THE KEY TO PRIORITIZATION

The quotation by Stephen Covey underlines how crucial it is to intentionally arrange our life around our most significant objectives and ideals. We must deliberately allocate time and attention to the things that genuinely matter rather than simply responding to what comes our way. We can choose how we spend our time consciously by setting priorities.

But seek first the kingdom of God and his righteousness, and all these things will be added to you, the Bible says. – **Matt. 6:33**. You might feel aligned and fulfilled by pursuing righteousness and giving the spiritual facets of our lives priority. Other facets of our lives flow more freely when our priorities are founded in our values.

The innovative businessman Elon Musk is renowned for his work on numerous challenging initiatives, including SpaceX, Tesla, Neuralink, and others. Musk's extraordinary capacity for setting priorities well is demonstrated by his ability to manage these companies while attending to a variety of duties.

By assigning time and resources to each project depending on its importance and impact, Musk keeps his concentration and balance. He can lead these initiatives at the same time because of his capacity for setting precise goals and surrounding himself with capable people. His undertakings are in line with these ideals since he places a high priority on creativity, sustainability, and the growth of humanity.

How to Establish Priorities and Achieving Balance

- ➢ Find your essential beliefs and use them as a compass to direct your actions and priorities.
- ➢ Make concrete, quantifiable, and time-bound goals for the various aspects of your life.
- ➢ Employ time blocking to ensure that you concentrate on the most important things by setting out certain time blocks for jobs and activities.
- ➢ Saying no to obligations that are not absolutely necessary that will help you protect your time and energy.
- ➢ Distribute jobs where you can, and give others the authority they need to carry out their duties well.

Achieving balance and setting priorities will enable us to live meaningful lives. Setting priorities involves focusing on what matters most, not on doing more. We may negotiate the difficulties of life with balance and purpose by planning our priorities and looking for alignment with our beliefs. Keep in mind that living harmoniously results from making decisions that are in line with your goals for achievement and fulfillment.

CELEBRATING SMALL WINS

Success is the sum of tiny efforts made repeatedly over time, according to the adage The Power of Small Efforts. (Robert Collier)

Over time, every little action we take to attain our goals adds up to big victories. The secret to maintaining motivation and attention is to acknowledge and value these little accomplishments.

 "He received a "well done, good and faithful servant" from his master. You have been trustworthy with a small amount, but I will give you lots to handle. Enter into your master's joy." – Matt. 25:23

This emphasizes the satisfaction and reward that result from being devoted and true to our work. Recognizing our fidelity in the tiny things spurs us to keep moving forward with diligence and dedication.

Tennis legend Serena Williams is a shining example of someone who pursued her goals with perseverance and determination. Williams encountered many difficulties throughout her career, including injuries and challenging opponents. But she never wavered in her commitment to improving her training, her abilities, or her quest of excellence.

Williams, despite the challenges she faced, appreciated each small success and growth along the road. She stayed motivated and steadfast to keep moving forward by appreciating each small step forward. With an unrivaled record of Grand Slam victories, she was able to establish herself as one of the greatest tennis players in history thanks to her mentality.

The Value of Recognizing Little Successes

- ❖ Momentum: Celebrating tiny victories gives us a boost in motivation and encourages us to keep up the good work.
- ❖ Recognizing accomplishments, no matter how minor, helps people feel more confident and self-assured.
- ❖ Encouragement for Perseverance: Seeing our progress motivates us to keep going despite difficulties.
- ❖ Enjoying little victories encourages a good perspective, which improves general wellbeing.
- ❖ Recognizing minor victories encourages thankfulness and enhances our ability to appreciate the path.

Recognizing minor victories helps us move toward achievement and fulfillment. Every little effort we make advances us and helps us get closer to our objectives. We inject joy, enthusiasm, and a positive outlook into our endeavor by enjoying these successes. Keep in mind that greatness is not attained through a single titanic act, but rather through a series of minor successes that are gratefully acknowledged and pursued with tenacity.

In "The Easy Thing," the significance of finding balance in life is emphasized as well as the value of simplicity in understanding complex circumstances. It emphasizes how important it is to make decisions based on one's principles and goals, inspiring readers to pursue personal growth and fulfillment.

It is to encourage you to approach life with curiosity, grit, and a dedication to lifelong learning. It is a manual that equips readers with the skills necessary to meet challenges head-on, get over roadblocks, and excel by appreciating the journey and each accomplishment along the way. Readers can alter their lives, have fun in the process, and build a meaningful and rewarding future by adopting the principles contained in this book.

Einleitung

In diesem E-Book werden wir uns eingehend mit dem Thema Geld beschäftigen und einen Vergleich zwischen den finanziellen Systemen von heute und früher ziehen. Insbesondere werden wir untersuchen, warum unser gegenwärtiges Geldsystem, das auf Zinsen und Zinseszinsen basiert, langfristig zum Scheitern verurteilt ist. Es ist wichtig, dieses Thema zu verstehen, da Geld eine zentrale Rolle in unserem Leben spielt und unser Wohlstand und unsere finanzielle Zukunft stark davon abhängen.

Kapitel 1: Die Entwicklung des Geldsystems

In diesem Kapitel werden wir einen kurzen Überblick über die Geschichte des Geldes geben und wie sich unser Geldsystem im Laufe der Zeit entwickelt hat. Von Tauschhandel zu Münzen und Banknoten bis hin zu digitalen Währungen haben sich die Formen des Geldes ständig verändert.

Kapitel 2: Das gegenwärtige Geldsystem

Hier werden wir das aktuelle Geldsystem genauer unter die Lupe nehmen, das auf Fiat-Währungen, Zentralbanken und einem Zinssystem basiert. Wir werden die Funktionsweise dieses Systems erläutern und seine Auswirkungen auf die Wirtschaft und die Gesellschaft diskutieren.

Kapitel 3: Die Bedeutung von Zinsen und Zinseszinsen

In diesem Kapitel werden wir uns intensiv mit dem Konzept der Zinsen und Zinseszinsen befassen und erklären, warum es so grundlegend ist. Wir werden auch erläutern, wie Zinsen in unserem gegenwärtigen Geldsystem funktionieren und welche Auswirkungen sie haben.

Kapitel 4: Die Probleme unseres gegenwärtigen Geldsystems

Wir werden in diesem Kapitel auf die Schwächen und Probleme unseres gegenwärtigen Geldsystems eingehen. Dazu gehören unter anderem die Verschuldungsspirale, die Ungleichheit, die Inflation und die Abhängigkeit von Zentralbanken.

Kapitel 5: Alternativen und Reformen

Um die Schwächen unseres gegenwärtigen Geldsystems zu beheben, werden wir in diesem Kapitel verschiedene Alternativen und Reformvorschläge diskutieren. Dazu gehören Ideen wie Vollgeldreform, Kryptowährungen, lokale Währungen und andere Ansätze zur Verbesserung des Geldsystems.

Kapitel 6: Die Zukunft des Geldes

Abschließend werden wir einen Blick in die Zukunft werfen und darüber spekulieren, wie sich das Geldsystem in den kommenden Jahren entwickeln könnte. Welche Veränderungen sind zu erwarten, und wie können wir uns auf diese Entwicklungen vorbereiten?

Fazit

In diesem E-Book haben wir das Thema Geld von verschiedenen Blickwinkeln aus betrachtet und insbesondere die Schwächen unseres gegenwärtigen Geldsystems analysiert. Es ist klar, dass unser derzeitiges System auf lange Sicht nicht nachhaltig ist. Es ist wichtig, sich dieser Problematik bewusst zu sein und